MW01243315

TINY BATTLEFIELDS

FIGHTING
POLIO

MARY COLSON

Gareth Stevens
PUBLISHING

Please visit our website, www.garethstevens.com. For a free color catalog of all our high-quality books, call toll free 1-800-542-2595 or fax 1-877-542-2596.

Colson, Mary.
Fighting Polio / by Mary Colson.
p. cm. -- (Tiny battlefields)
Includes index.
ISBN 978-1-4824-1358-8 (pbk.)
ISBN 978-1-4824-1313-7 (6-pack)
ISBN 978-1-4824-1435-6 (library binding)
1. Poliomyelitis -- Juvenile literature. I. Colson, Mary. II. Title.
RC180.1 C65 2015
616.8--d23

Library of Congress Cataloging-in-Publication Data

First Edition

Published in 2015 by
Gareth Stevens Publishing
111 East 14th Street, Suite 349
New York, NY 10003

© 2015 Gareth Stevens Publishing

Produced by: Calcium, www.calciumcreative.co.uk
Designed by: Simon Borrough
Edited by: Sarah Eason and Jennifer Sanderson
Picture research by: Rachel Blount

Photo credits: Cover: Dreamstime: Krishnacreations; Inside: Centers for Disease Control and Prevention: 11, 34, Charles Farmer 8, Mary Hilpertshauser 9; Dreamstime: Carrienelson1 17, Alan Gignoux 14, Junpinzon 4, Krishnacreations 1, Samrat35 45, Yunxiang987 3, 42; Flickr: Jean-Marc Giboux/RIBI Image Library 39, RIBI Image Library 41, Damien du Toit 35, U.S. Mission photo by Eric Bridiers 38; Library of Congress: Al Ravenna 12; Massachusetts Institute of Technology: 30; Shutterstock: 7, 20, 29, 43, Anyaivanova 31, Asianet-Pakistan 5, 18, 22, 23, 24, 44, Hector Conesa 16, Creations 6, Eric Fahrner 13, Fpolat69 15, Sadik Gulec 36, Kojoku 32, Lorimer Images 25, Meunierd 10, Molekuul.be 27, 28, Andrii Muzyka 26, Patrick Poendl 21, Paul Prescott 40, Gary Yim 33, Zurijeta 37.

Printed in the United States of America

CPSIA compliance information: Batch #CS15GS: For further information contact Gareth Stevens, New York, New York at 1-800-542-2595.

CONTENTS

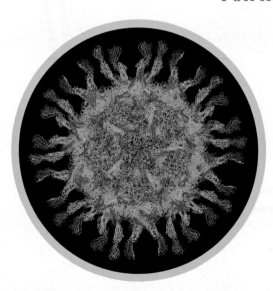

CHAPTER 1: WAGING WAR

All over the world, the most vulnerable people are fighting a deadly virus. It is a battle that many thought had already been won. In many countries, the fight is short and is won by a simple childhood vaccine. Elsewhere, however, the tiny polio virus is starting to take hold once more, just when scientists believed it had been destroyed for good.

ATTACKING THE YOUNG

Poliomyelitis, or polio, is a highly contagious virus that can lead to breathing problems, paralysis, and even death. The virus attacks the spinal cord and destroys the body's nerve cells. Polio affects mainly children under the age of five. One in 20 infections will lead to permanent paralysis and around 10 percent of these patients will die because their lungs, the body's breathing muscles, simply cannot move.

In some parts of the world, polio sufferers are forced to beg for food to survive.

No Cure

Polio is a crippling, deadly virus that can change lives forever. There is no known cure for it. As long as one person is infected somewhere in the world, the virus can fight back and an epidemic can happen at any moment.

A Global Fight

In 2012, the World Health Organization (WHO) reported that there were 223 cases of polio worldwide. In 2013, that number had risen to 347, with the majority of the new cases in Nigeria, Somalia, and Pakistan. WHO also reported cases in Syria, a country that had previously been polio-free thanks to a vaccination program.

"WHO wants to get rid of polio completely and had got pretty close until recent outbreaks. The fact that most of those infected do not display symptoms, but can still spread the disease, makes it a very hard virus to get rid of. It is like fighting an invisible enemy."

Professor Martin Eichner, University of Tubingen, Germany

A Deadly Enemy

The tiny polio virus thrives in areas with poor sanitation. Outbreaks of the virus are usually in places with poor hygiene and inadequate medical facilities. Contaminated water or food or direct contact with an infected person can cause polio. How does the virus take over? What are the signs and symptoms of the virus, and how can medicine tackle this tiny enemy?

Invisible Intruder

Very often, people infected with polio display no symptoms to begin with. When symptoms do appear, they differ depending on what type of polio virus the person has. The polio virus can affect different nerve cells that may or may not cause paralysis. Nonparalytic polio usually begins with flu-like symptoms that can last for a few days or a few weeks. More severe symptoms include muscle spasms and meningitis. Paralytic polio starts in a similar way to nonparalytic polio, but develops into far more serious symptoms such as severe muscle pain, loss of reflexes, floppy limbs, difficulty swallowing and breathing, and, finally, paralysis. If the polio virus attaches to brain cells, brain damage can also occur.

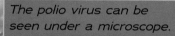
The polio virus can be seen under a microscope.

6

On the Battlefield

Viruses are microorganisms. When they enter the human body, the immune system tries to fight them off. Viruses survive by finding a living host cell and multiplying quickly. The human immune system recognizes the intruder and attacks it with billions of white blood cells. If a virus multiplies itself more quickly than the immune system can respond, it will take over. In many countries, children are vaccinated against polio. This means they are given a low dose of the disease so that their bodies can recognize the virus and build up resistance.

Viruses infect our bodies and begin their attack. The polio virus targets nerve cells specifically.

DIAGNOSING THE ENEMY

Doctors diagnose polio by analyzing saliva, stool samples, or spinal fluid. If a person's immune system is fighting a virus, the test results will show a high number of white blood cells. The body's protein levels are also higher than usual if the patient has contracted polio. Once a diagnosis is certain, doctors need to know what type of polio the patient has. "Vaccine" polio means that the virus is a strain of the type used in polio vaccines. "Wild" polio means that the person has caught the virus from nature. It is estimated that for every reported case of wild polio, there are anywhere between 200 to 3,000 contagious carriers of the virus.

A HISTORIC THREAT

Polio is a very old disease. In fact, there are ancient Egyptian hieroglyphs of people with withered limbs and children walking with canes. In the past, polio was very common worldwide. In the late eighteenth century, doctors first recognized a virus that affected people's legs and their ability to walk.

BREAKTHROUGH!

In 1955, Jonas Salk created the first successful polio vaccine, which scientists thought would be the beginning of the end for the virus. There are now only three countries where polio remains a serious problem: Nigeria, Pakistan, and Afghanistan. In these countries, conflict, poverty, poor hygiene, or political issues have so far prevented a total destruction of polio.

This photograph, taken in 1963, shows US physical therapists helping child polio victims to exercise as part of their treatment.

On the Battlefield

In 1952, the United States suffered a polio epidemic. More than 58,000 cases were reported and nearly half of the victims died or were permanently disabled. In 1955, a virologist named Jonas Salk announced that his polio vaccine had been successfully trialed using 220,000 volunteers. The Salk vaccine is also known as the IPV vaccine, which stands for inactivated polio virus vaccine. Two doses of the vaccine are usually enough for people to develop enough antibodies to fight off the virus if they become infected at a later date. In 1962, Albert Sabin developed an oral polio vaccine (OPV). A single dose of Sabin's vaccine gives immunity against most forms of polio. Today, Sabin's OPV is used worldwide in the fight against polio.

TOWARD A POLIO-FREE WORLD

Mass vaccination programs are helping WHO win the battle for a polio-free world. In 1994, the United States and the rest of the Americas were declared "polio free." Europe followed in 2002. Nigeria, Pakistan, and Afghanistan continue to have a major polio problem and this can cause problems for nearby countries, too. For example, the African countries of Somalia and Chad have reported new cases and scientists have linked these to a strain of the virus present in neighboring Nigeria.

In 1963, this poster was used throughout the United States to encourage people to vaccinate against polio.

WHO IS AT RISK?

Very young children, people with weak immune systems, and those who have not been vaccinated are particularly at risk from polio. Scientists who work with the polio virus in laboratories are also vulnerable and must take special precautions when handling the virus.

"When I was about nine, I had polio, and people were very frightened for their children, so you tended to be isolated. I was paralyzed for a while, so I watched television."

Francis Ford Coppola, movie director

Kenya has a high poverty rate and many people live in slums. These can be polio breeding grounds because of poor hygiene.

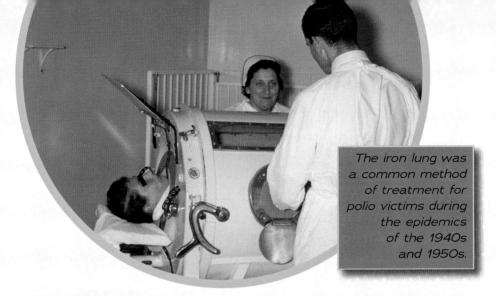

The iron lung was a common method of treatment for polio victims during the epidemics of the 1940s and 1950s.

TREATMENT OPTIONS

Each patient develops polio symptoms differently because the virus attacks a variety of nerves and muscles. For example, a victim may take medicine to stop muscle pain or antibiotics to cure other infections. Other prescriptions include moderate exercise and a healthy diet. Physical therapy is usually part of the treatment for polio, to help patients learn to work their wasted muscles. Some people wear leg braces called calipers and special shoes to support their legs.

THE IRON LUNG

Today, if a patient suffers from lung paralysis and cannot breathe properly, he or she is put on a portable ventilator. There are also special jacket-ventilators that inflate the lung muscles. In the past, patients were put into machines called "iron lungs." Like a modern ventilator, this device pushed and pulled the lung muscles to help with breathing. Patients could spend up to a week in the iron lung. When the polio epidemic was at its worst in North America in the 1940s and 1950s, there were wards of polio patients in iron lungs.

WATER CURES

US President Franklin D. Roosevelt had polio. In adulthood, he became sick and subsequently walked with two sticks or used a wheelchair. He visited a treatment center in Georgia called Warm Springs. Doctors believed hydrotherapy (water treatment) in warm, mineral-rich water eased muscles and restored strength.

CHAPTER 2: A GLOBAL BATTLE

All over the world, polio still infects people and attacks their immune systems. Although the disease has remained the same, its treatment has changed over the years.

Elizabeth Kenny revolutionized polio treatment worldwide during the 1940s.

THE KENNY METHOD

Elizabeth Kenny was an Australian nurse who was at the forefront of polio treatment in the first half of the twentieth century. Her method of treating patients was different from the method that many medical practitioners at the time believed was best. Kenny said that patients needed to exercise muscles affected by polio rather than having them immobilized in braces, splints, or plaster casts. She traveled throughout North America and Europe demonstrating her treatment methods and setting up clinics.

PHYSICAL THERAPY AND TREATMENT

Kenny's methods were the beginning of modern physical therapy treatments. Current physical therapy treatment for polio involves targeting and exercising specific muscle groups in an attempt to rehabilitate them. Physical therapy is also used to rehabilitate the patient's neural pathways. Neural pathways are part of the body's central nervous system. If a pathway is damaged because of polio, physical therapy can help create a new pathway to recover normal movement in the patient's muscles.

Today, in addition to physical therapy, most polio patients are given drugs to limit their pain and to boost their immune system, but there are no medicines that kill off the virus completely. Therefore, much of the treatment is to limit the impact of the symptoms.

"All you need is over 90 percent of children to have the vaccine drop three times and the disease stops spreading. The number of cases eventually goes to zero. When we started, we had over 400,000 children a year being paralyzed and we are now down to under 1,000 cases a year."

Bill Gates,
cofounder of the Bill and Melinda Gates Foundation

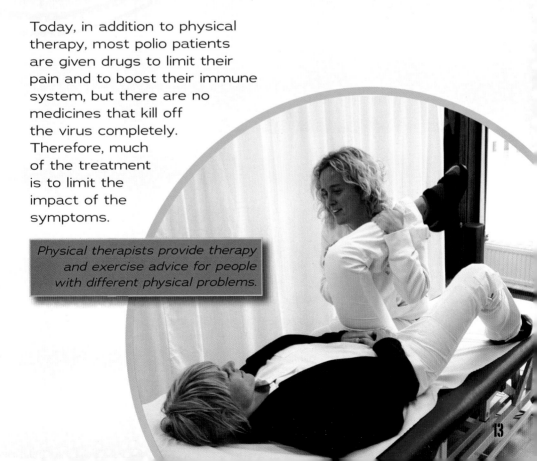

Physical therapists provide therapy and exercise advice for people with different physical problems.

POLIO AROUND THE WORLD

WHO estimates that there are 10 to 20 million polio survivors worldwide, with around 250,000 in the United States. At its peak, the virus infected hundreds of thousands of people each year. Today, that number is vastly reduced thanks to vaccinations and better sanitation, but there remain areas of the world still at risk of a polio epidemic.

CRISIS IN AFRICA

For many years, the countries of central Africa have been ravaged by conflict and poverty. Low sanitation levels, famine, and lack of vaccinations have left the population weak and vulnerable to the polio virus. In 2012, polio cases in Nigeria, Chad, Niger, Congo, Kenya, and Somalia made up 75 percent of the worldwide cases.

Raising awareness is vital to stop the spread of polio. Here, campaigners in Uganda march to educate parents about the importance of immunizing their children.

War in Syria has disrupted food and medical supplies and created millions of refugees.

WAR BREEDS DISEASE

Afghanistan has suffered from almost continuous conflict for many years. It is also a vast country with some people living in very remote places. Both of these issues make vaccinating children very challenging. On the borders of Afghanistan is Pakistan, and these two countries have reported more than 100 polio cases in the last year alone. The virus is highly contagious and WHO is extremely concerned that the poor hygiene and severely disrupted medical services in both countries make a perfect breeding ground for a polio epidemic.

WAR IN SYRIA

By 2013, the ongoing civil war in Syria had led to a breakdown of the country's health and sanitation infrastructures. With broken water and sewage pipes and a semicollapsed hospital system struggling to cope with the battle-wounded, the conditions are perfect for a rapid spread of polio. By the end of 2013, 13 cases of polio had left their victims partially paralyzed.

On the Battlefield

Large numbers of Syrian refugees are moving to other countries to escape the conflict. This means the disease could soon spread across Europe. WHO and the United Nations Children's Fund (UNICEF) are conducting a huge campaign to inoculate more than 22 million children against polio in Syria and six other Middle Eastern countries.

LIVING WITH POLIO

All over the world, there are millions of people who have had polio and live with the consequences of the virus. How badly they are affected by the virus depends on the number of nerve cells that were damaged by polio.

LIMITED OPPORTUNITIES?

In countries with good medical care and family and social support for infected people, life for polio sufferers can continue in a positive way. For less fortunate sufferers, life opportunities are severely limited. In developing countries where there is less money and less developed medical and social welfare systems, people disabled by polio are often left without jobs. Sometimes they are cast out from their communities because people think they cannot work, earn money, marry, or contribute to society.

In Varanasi, India, hundreds of people are forced to beg because polio has left them unable to work.

FAMOUS FACES OF POLIO

Having polio does not always stop people from following their dreams and having exciting lives. The singers Neil Young and Joni Mitchell both suffered from polio when they were children. Itzhak Perlman is considered one of the world's greatest violinists. He contracted polio at the age of four but he recovered and taught himself to walk with crutches. The writer Arthur C. Clark, the painter Frida Kahlo, and the photographer Dorothea Lange all contracted polio as children and went on to have hugely successful careers.

POST-POLIO SYNDROME

For many people around the world, polio is essentially a disease of the past. However, between 25 to 50 percent of people who have had polio develop a condition called post-polio syndrome (PPS). Not much is understood about PPS but chronic tiredness, joint pain, sleeping problems, feeling the cold, breathing difficulties, and weak muscles are some of the symptoms. At present, there is no test for PPS and it sometimes takes many years to develop. In some cases, patients develop the syndrome 30 or 40 years after they had polio. The longest recorded gap is 71 years after the initial polio infection.

The effects of polio are long-lasting— leading musician Itzhak Perlman will always rely on crutches and a mobility chair.

ON THE FRONTLINE

When there is a polio outbreak, it is not just doctors, physical therapists, and nurses who are involved. Often, professors and scientific researchers work with them to study how the disease affects people. This knowledge then helps them to develop new care or improved support systems and, potentially, even new treatments. Other front line workers include the polio mobilizers who go from home to home, educating parents and persuading them to allow their children to be vaccinated.

HELPING HAND

Many charities are involved with polio prevention and treatment programs. Staff from Nottingham University and Nottingham University Hospitals in the United Kingdom started the Uganda Polio Project. The project involves taking used and unwanted equipment to Uganda for use there. Uganda has no national policy for helping the disabled, so medics, teachers, and volunteers go to the country to treat hundreds of patients.

THE DEVELOPMENT OF PHYSICAL THERAPY

The polio epidemic in the United States in the 1940s and 1950s meant that new ways of treating the patients needed to be developed.

Pakistan's Polio Task Force is working toward eradicating polio in the country.

Physical therapy became the latest word in easing some of the worst symptoms of the virus. A physical therapist works to help improve movement and body function if it is damaged. He or she assesses the whole body and how it should work, and gives patients particular exercises to do.

Today, physical therapists work all over the world treating many different kinds of pain and illness. Both polio and PPS patients require specialist physical therapy techniques including specific exercises and massage. These are designed to help improve flexibility, increase muscle power, improve stamina, improve circulation, and help to develop some nerve control in affected body areas.

This microscopic image shows muscle tissue affected and damaged by polio.

"Some families do not allow us to vaccinate their children . . . The main challenge for social mobilizers and the vaccinators is that families sometimes think that the vaccine is not good for their children . . . the vaccinators and social mobilizers have to help them understand why it is so important to vaccinate every child in every campaign and we have to convince them that the vaccine is safe."

Polio Mobilizer, Khandahar Province, Afghanistan

POLIO MOBILIZERS

In Afghanistan, local people volunteer to act as polio mobilizers. They are trained by local health-care professionals and international aid organizations. Their job is to go from home to home to mark dots on the front of each home to represent the number of children in the household. Health care professionals then vaccinate all the children in the following days.

CHAPTER 3: THE POVERTY TRAP

Polio affects many different areas of life in a community, including people's ability to earn money. For millions of people in certain hotspot countries, the poverty trap makes them vulnerable to infection. What can science do to protect people in poor countries, and how are medical breakthroughs having a positive effect on lives?

India has carried out a highly successful polio vaccination program in recent years.

On the Battlefield

Polio is now endemic in three countries only: Nigeria, Pakistan, and Afghanistan. Endemic means that there are ongoing cases and infections of the disease. Polio is so contagious that WHO considers a single case of it an epidemic because of how rapidly the disease can spread. Nigeria, Pakistan, and Afghanistan have great problems getting vaccines to the people who need it. In April 2013, the Global Polio Eradication Initiative (GPEI), supported by WHO, outlined a plan to eliminate polio through a mass vaccination program in these three countries.

ONLY PREVENTION IS POSSIBLE

Polio can be prevented only by vaccination so a continual program of vaccinating babies must occur if polio is to become eradicated. In vast countries with huge mountain ranges, such as Pakistan and Afghanistan, identifying, locating, and then reaching people who have not been vaccinated is an enormous challenge. Nigeria has many nomadic people, too. This further complicates the attempt to vaccinate everyone. WHO works with governments, local authorities, community groups, and even tribal leaders in its effort to reach everyone.

KEEPING WATCH

Scientists warn that people can never let down their guard against the polio virus. If an outbreak occurs in a country that has previously had no cases, then even people who have been vaccinated are not always immune to the disease. For example, in 2013, the polio virus was found in sewage samples in Israel, a country that has been polio-free for many years. The Israeli ministry of health set about boosting immunity in both children and adults by administering an additional dose of the vaccine.

21

A WINNABLE WAR?

In any country where there is poor sanitation or low hygiene, the wild polio virus will pose a potential deadly threat. The virus is spread through person-to-person contact, mostly through children, and enters the body through the mouth before multiplying in the intestine. It then moves into the bloodstream and attacks the central nervous system where neuron cells are destroyed. When body waste is passed, the virus enters the environment in feces. If food or water is contaminated, the virus can spread quickly through a community.

Providing clean water and good hygiene is vital if the polio virus is to be beaten.

"As long as the virus is alive and people are moving with the virus, it will spread as people move. And when it lands in places where immunization and sanitation are not in place, that is where the setbacks will take place."

Dr. Hamid Jafari, director of WHO's Global Polio Eradication Initiative

Global Challenge

UNICEF is working with medical professionals in its Stop Transmission of Polio (STOP) campaign. Its medical volunteers are going into Nigeria, Afghanistan, and Pakistan to vaccinate children in communities that have been weakened by conflict, poverty, low hygiene, or poor sanitation. With a decrease of 99 percent in polio cases between 1988 and 2012, the STOP campaign and other initiatives have been successful. However, until the last country is declared polio-free, the virus could rear its ugly head again.

Education Is Vital

In developing countries, many parents are uneducated and do not know how to protect their children from the devastating polio virus. Health-care workers in Pakistan and Afghanistan run workshops at which new mothers and fathers are told about polio and why they should have their child vaccinated. The difficulty in educating everyone about the dangers of polio in huge countries such as Pakistan is made worse by the mountainous landscape, poor rural road networks, and unreliable communications networks.

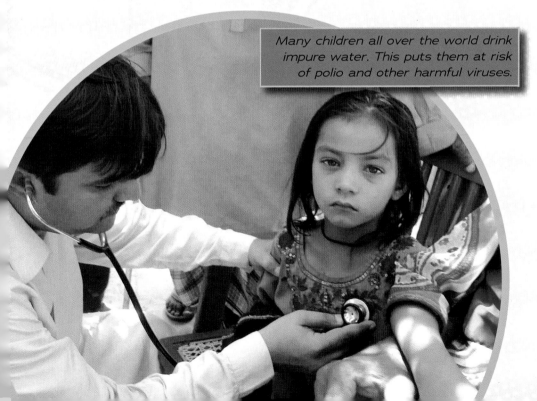

Many children all over the world drink impure water. This puts them at risk of polio and other harmful viruses.

POLIO AND POLITICS

At the beginning of the twenty-first century, the world is tantalizingly close to eradicating polio. Science has made huge strides toward prevention and post-infection therapies. However, the last strongholds of endemic polio are in some of the most politically unstable places in the world. All too often, public health becomes a bargaining tool.

FRONTLINE MEDICINE

A quick injection or a couple of drops of medicine on the tongue may seem simple to people in developed countries where there is adequate health care. In other countries, however, it is not so easy. One of the biggest challenges to health care workers is violence. For example, in Pakistan in December 2012, Taliban fighters shot dead nine UNICEF health-care workers as they went from house to house to administer polio vaccines. In January 2013, six aid workers and a doctor were also killed as they tried to vaccinate children.

Pakistan's antipolio campaign aims to vaccinate every child in the country against polio.

A Question of Belief

The Taliban believed that the polio vaccine would make the children sterile. A similar case occurred in 2003, when a number of Nigeria's states refused to administer the polio vaccination to children. The leaders believed that the vaccines were tampered with and that the dose would make people infertile. As a result, millions of children went unprotected against the deadly virus, just as they did in Pakistan. Parents who wanted to vaccinate their children had to travel to different states or pay for the vaccine at a private clinic.

Children in Nigeria are at risk of catching polio because of religious fears about the vaccine.

The Impact of Not Vaccinating

By not vaccinating in Nigeria, there has been a rise of polio cases across 10 countries where polio had previously been eradicated. Nigeria now has 70 percent of the world's polio cases. Doctors working for WHO are currently working with the Nigerian central government to administer vaccines nationwide, but already more children have died or become crippled.

"This rise in polio is mainly due to nonvaccination. Where immunization is high we don't find the disease there."

Dr. Abdullahi Walla, WHO surveillance officer for disease control for Nigeria's northwest region

CHAPTER 4: SCIENTIFIC WEAPONS

Scientists already know a great deal about the polio virus but questions still remain. For example, why does the virus seem to favor motor neuron cells over other cells in the central nervous system? Other human cells have receptors that fit the polio virus so research is being conducted into why the virus acts as it does.

Nerve cells are also called neurons. They carry messages to muscles and organs around the body through the nervous system.

TRANSMISSION CHAINS

Scientists explain viruses being passed from one person to another, or from a source to a person, as a transmission route. If the virus is then passed on to someone else or many people, it is called a transmission chain. One of the ways scientists attack the polio virus is to disrupt this chain as early as possible to limit its impact. The difficulty with the polio virus is locating the beginning of the chain because around 95 percent of all infections cause no symptoms. Furthermore, not showing any symptoms can still spread the virus because it is shed in the patient's stool.

ON ALERT

In all but three countries in the world, polio transmission has been successfully interrupted. However, not all children around the world are immunized so the polio virus could be easily imported to a polio-free country and spread rapidly. If this happens, WHO estimates there will be 200,000 new cases every year within 10 years.

"Scenarios for polio being introduced into the United States are easy to imagine, and the disease could get a foothold if we do not maintain high vaccination rates. For example, an unvaccinated US resident could travel abroad and become infected before returning home.
A visitor to the US could travel here while infected. The point is, one person infected with polio is all it takes to start the spread of polio to others if they are not protected by vaccination."

Dr. Greg Wallace,
National Center for Immunization
and Respiratory Diseases

SCIENTIFIC CHALLENGES

Doctors can treat some of the symptoms of polio, but they cannot cure it. Antibiotics do not work because polio is caused by a virus and not bacteria. The virus does not naturally reproduce in any other species so researchers cannot observe how it functions elsewhere. However, researchers at the University of Liverpool in England have been studying a new virus that is closely related to polio: Enterovirus 71. This virus causes similar devastating symptoms to polio and has spread across Asia. To help fight polio, the Liverpool-based scientists have developed tests that can help doctors predict how the virus may affect any individual patient. The doctors then know which patient will develop serious brain infection as a result of the virus and so start to treat it early.

The polio virus has similar symptoms to Enterovirus 71. Doctors are studying the virus to help them better understand the polio virus.

MICROBIOLOGICAL BATTLEFIELDS

All viruses have a weak point, a chink in their armor. Scientists and researchers study them until they find the weakness and then find ways of exploiting it. This process can take many years, even many decades. Today, scientists have a vast amount of knowledge about deoxyribonucleic acid (DNA) and the human immune system. This is helping them limit the effects of polio and slowly win the war on the microbiological battlefield.

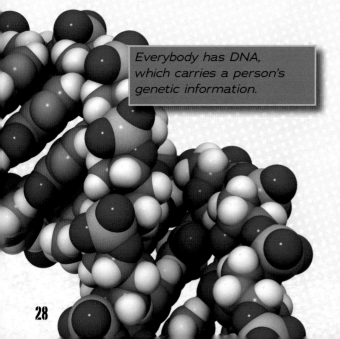

Everybody has DNA, which carries a person's genetic information.

THE VIRAL STRUCTURE OF POLIO

A single particle of the polio virus measures no more than 30 nanometers across: that is about 0.000000118 inch (0.0000003 cm)! On its own, it is harmless, but once it finds a host cell, this tiny viral particle can wreak deadly destruction. The virus is made up of six main elements: carbon, hydrogen, nitrogen, oxygen, phosphorus, and sulfur. Each viral particle contains ribonucleic acid (RNA) surrounded by a protein shell known as a capsid. RNA is a large molecule that carries genetic information. The viral particle attaches itself to the cell receptors of a motor neuron cell. It is then the virus starts to reproduce itself at a frightening speed.

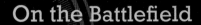

On the Battlefield

Scientists know how the polio virus behaves, changes, and mutates, and they also know its genetic code. It is now possible to create the polio virus (and other viruses such as smallpox) in a laboratory. This is called synthesizing. A synthetic virus could, in time, be altered to create new vaccines or to develop a new type of gene therapy for polio victims.

The central nervous system is made up of the brain and spinal cord. The spinal cord runs along a person's spine.

POLIO TYPES

There are three types of polio virus: 1, 2, and 3. Type 1 is the most common and the most severe. This is also called spinal polio. The virus infection causes inflammation of the nerve cells and can lead to paralysis. Type 2 is also called bulbar polio. This virus strain destroys bulbar nerves in the brain. When the nerves are affected, it can cause breathing, swallowing, and speaking problems. Type 3 is also called bulbospinal polio, and this attacks the nerves that control the lungs, making breathing and swallowing extremely difficult. Testing for all three types involves blood tests, stool samples, and a spinal tap, which is when a needle is inserted into the spinal cord to take a sample of fluid. Scientists can then see if the patient has antibodies to the polio virus or a high white blood count, which indicates that he or she has polio.

TESTING TREATMENTS

Many of the financial and scientific resources available for polio are used to help vaccinate the world's children. Today, scientists are developing new drugs to help patients who have caught the virus to recover. These new drugs are just some of the latest treatments available.

On the Battlefield

Most bacterial infections can be treated with antibiotics, but now there is hope that one day viruses such as polio may be able to be treated in a similar way. Researchers at the Massachusetts Institute of Technology (MIT) have been developing a new drug that could treat viral infections such as influenza (the flu), colds, and even more deadly viruses such as Ebola and polio. The new drug can identify cells that have been infected by any type of virus. It then kills those cells to end the infection. In tests, the drug has proven effective against cells containing the polio virus without harming uninfected cells. In time, if human trials are successful, the drug could be used not just to cure polio but also to combat other life-threatening viruses.

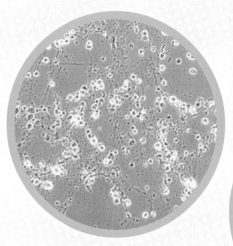

The image above left shows human cells that are infected with the flu virus. The image above right shows human cells in which the flu virus has been destroyed by a new antiviral drug.

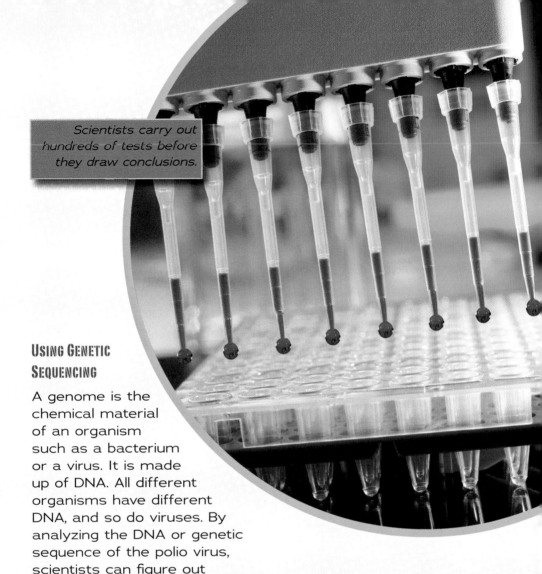

USING GENETIC SEQUENCING

A genome is the chemical material of an organism such as a bacterium or a virus. It is made up of DNA. All different organisms have different DNA, and so do viruses. By analyzing the DNA or genetic sequence of the polio virus, scientists can figure out where an outbreak started. Once this is known, targeted immunization can take place to limit the spread of the disease. This means that only vulnerable children in the immediate community would be vaccinated to begin with. This system was used in India to great effect and could also be used in the countries where polio remains a threat.

PREVENTION IS CHEAPER THAN CURE

It is far cheaper to vaccinate children to establish immunity and prevent a disease than spend millions of dollars researching a possible cure. For this reason, it seems unlikely that a cure will be developed for polio unless it occurs as a result of other research.

COUNTING CASES AND MAPPING TRENDS

The GPEI is run by WHO, national governments, UNICEF, Rotary International, and the US Centers for Disease Control and Prevention (CDC). It targets 200 countries and has 20 million volunteers. To date, 2.5 billion children have been immunized, and polio cases have decreased by more than 99 percent since 1988, from an estimated 350,000 cases then to 223 reported cases in 2012. The GPEI has just one goal: to eradicate polio worldwide.

TREND MAPPING

Scientists at WHO monitor new polio cases closely. They produce maps to track the virus spread, and a weekly report is given to field officers in affected regions. Surveillance, response, and containment are the three main prongs of attack to prevent a polio epidemic. Surveillance means recording all new cases and seeing where the virus is spreading. Response and containment are concerned with treating the patients and trying to limit the possible and predicted transmission routes of the virus. This might mean infected patients are removed from their

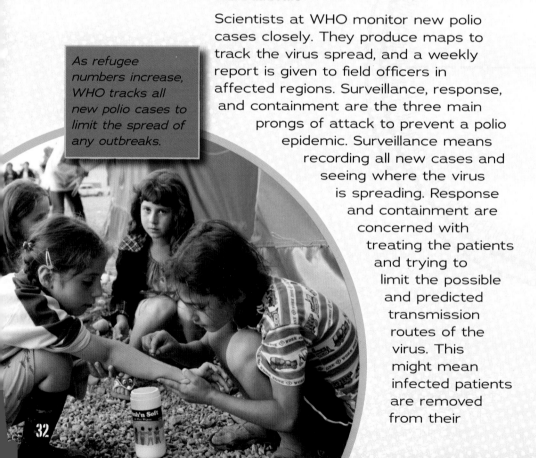

As refugee numbers increase, WHO tracks all new polio cases to limit the spread of any outbreaks.

communities for a time to help prevent further cases.

REACHING THE LAST FEW

One of the big challenges in eradicating polio is immunizing children in migrant populations. Millions of people around the world live in mobile communities. This means they do not have a fixed settlement but move around depending on the season and on job opportunities. They may even move to a country where polio has been eradicated. If they are carriers of the virus and other unvaccinated children are present, a new outbreak could occur—with deadly consequences. Children in conflict zones are also very vulnerable because conflict disrupts many aspects of life including medical services. The cost of reaching the last few children affected by polio is estimated to be hundreds of millions of dollars.

Children in conflict zones or poor communities are at higher risk of catching polio.

"Wild viruses and wildfires have two things in common. If neglected, they can spread out of control. If handled properly, they can be stamped out for good. Today, the flame of polio is near extinction—but sparks in three countries threaten to ignite a global blaze. Now is the moment to act."

Ban Ki-moon, secretary-general of the United Nations

Chapter 5: Raising Awareness About Polio

Keeping the fight against polio in the public eye is vital if the last strongholds of the disease are to be broken. Charities and campaigners raise awareness and publicize the need for funds to finish the global vaccination process that was begun more than 50 years ago. With WHO and the UN at the heart of the process, and huge donations from charitable foundations such as the Bill and Melinda Gates Foundation, eradicating polio is finally starting to appear possible.

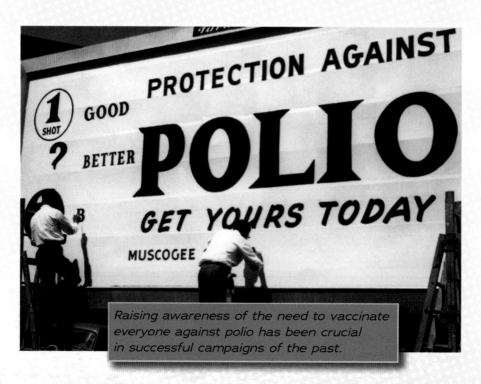

Raising awareness of the need to vaccinate everyone against polio has been crucial in successful campaigns of the past.

"The last pockets of this disease are the hardest and the most costly to reach."

Margaret Chan,
WHO director general

EVERY LAST CHILD

The most expensive children to reach are those in conflict zones or very remote areas. To reach these children often involves a risky journey by helicopter or traveling on tracks into mountains. A further complication is keeping the vaccine at the right temperature. Ideally, the polio vaccine should be kept at between 35 and 46 degrees Fahrenheit (2 and 8°C). In a country with a warm climate, such as Nigeria, expensive portable refrigerators are used, but they can break on rough journeys. The vaccine should also be protected from light. If these conditions are not met, the vaccine will not work.

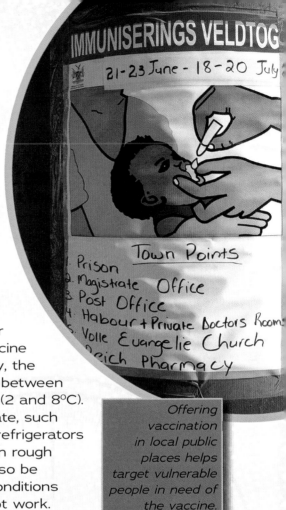

Offering vaccination in local public places helps target vulnerable people in need of the vaccine.

CAMPAIGN PROGRAM

Chad is next to Nigeria. Many people cross between the two countries for work and for personal reasons. Chad has had an enormous polio problem, coupled with a lack of understanding about the importance of vaccinating children. UNICEF started a campaign to make Chad polio-free and immunize all the children there. Great progress has been made, with immunizations rising and polio cases falling, despite the threat of a strain of the virus traveling from Nigeria. The campaign focuses on educating people about the importance of polio vaccination.

KNOWLEDGE IS POWER

Before Jonas Salk developed his vaccine, polio was the number one cause of disability in the United States. Fewer than two generations later, the United States is polio-free. Scientific knowledge, public and political will, and education about the disease meant that parents were happy to trust the vaccine to prevent the disease. However, this story has not been repeated in every country, and there are still places where polio outbreaks occur.

RISING NUMBERS

The GPEI estimates that there are more than 1 million children in East Africa alone who have not been vaccinated against polio. In Nigeria, some parents refuse to let their children be vaccinated unless the family receives additional benefits such as money or food. In Somalia, vaccination teams are unable to reach all children because of civil war. Some military leaders even prevent food and medicine getting through to their enemies' children.

Food and medicine are used as a weapon of war in Somalia. There, people survive on aid packages.

TAKING CONTROL: A TALE OF TWO COUNTRIES

Saudi Arabia and India are not usually considered very similar, but they have both taken bold measures to beat polio. Saudi Arabia is the home of Mecca, a holy place for Muslim pilgrims from all over the world. Saudi Arabia is polio-free so the authorities have taken the step of vaccinating people when they arrive in the country on pilgrimage. Equally, India has shown great leadership on polio eradication and surprised many international health bodies by achieving zero polio cases. After huge public education campaigns about the virus, virtually every Indian child was tracked and vaccinated over a period of 10 years. Before this, almost 1,000 Indian children a day were paralyzed because of polio. The challenge now facing WHO, UNICEF, GPEI, and other organizations is to ensure that these lessons translate into global polio eradication.

"India's accomplishment in eradicating polio is the most impressive global health success I've ever seen . . . India's success offers a script for winning some of the world's most difficult battles in every area of human welfare."

Bill Gates

Thousands of people visit Mecca each year as part of a pilgrimage. Vaccination of the pilgrims ensures that polio does not spread to Saudi Arabia.

Celebrity, Charity, and Campaigning

Before Jonas Salk created the polio vaccine, the virus was a threat to millions of children. Epidemics in the United States, Europe, and Australasia helped focus scientific resources and money into producing a vaccine. Today, the near-eradication of the virus means that the campaign is much more targeted on the polio hotspots that remain. It might seem as if the fight is won and that there is no need to campaign, but until everyone is vaccinated, the battle must continue.

Spreading the Message

Every year, October 24 is World Polio Day. On this day, there are events to raise awareness about the continuing fight against polio. Celebrity polio survivors, UNICEF spokespeople, and politicians give lectures, presentations, and speeches, and present television commercials about the final push to eradicate polio for good. Rotary International also runs a polio-eradication campaign called "This Close" with ambassadors such as Bill Gates and Jack Nicklaus. The campaign raises money for vaccination programs as well as awareness for the final battle against polio.

Bill Gates is a leading figure of and financial contributor to the international polio-eradication campaign.

Polio vaccination is an ongoing objective in India.

"I had polio when I was 13. I started feeling stiff, my joints ached, and over a two-week period I lost my coordination and 20 pounds."

Jack Nicklaus, champion golfer

LIFE AFTER POLIO

In polio-endemic countries, the sight of victims in wheelchairs, on crutches, or wearing leg braces is a familiar sight. There, the power of the polio virus is all too clear to see. Children and adults with deformed limbs are often forced to beg on the streets to survive. Polio Children is a charity that works with child polio victims to give them more life opportunities. The charity provides education and vocational training programs as well as taking care of victims' medical needs.

CHAPTER 6: FUTURE DIAGNOSIS

With a dramatic decrease in worldwide polio cases but an alarming rise in new cases in countries that had been polio-free, what does the future hold?

"It's important to put the issue of setbacks into the context of the program and recognize that progress continues. These outbreaks highlight the importance of eliminating the virus in the remaining endemic countries."

Dr. Hamid Jafari,
GPEI director

IT CAN BE DONE

Polio is being targeted so precisely because, like smallpox, it is a disease that can be completely eradicated. It is not yet possible to wipe out many diseases because scientific weapons are not yet powerful enough to fight them. However, polio is different because an effective vaccine exists. Eradicating polio would be beneficial to everyone and no child would ever need to suffer polio paralysis again. Health services in many countries have been developed to fight polio. These infrastructures of clinics, doctors, and patient monitoring

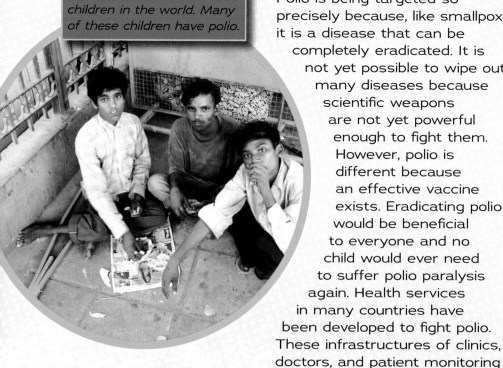

India has the largest population of street children in the world. Many of these children have polio.

are now being used to help patients fight other diseases such as measles and HIV/AIDS.

A Cautionary Tale

One of the biggest challenges facing researchers and campaigners in developed countries is keeping the fight against polio in the public eye. Most of the news about polio is about outbreaks in conflict areas or about cases in Africa. As a result, the need to remain vaccinated can become overlooked. While polio has been eradicated in most developed countries, the virus is still classed as an epidemic in a few key countries because it can spread so easily and with devastating effect. Public awareness and education must remain a top priority. Knowledge of how the virus can be spread and how to protect children against it needs to be combined with outreach programs to make sure that even those people living in remote regions are vaccinated. If this happens, the end of polio could be within humanity's grasp.

This young polio victim in Thailand has received treatment provided by Rotary International, improving her chances of recovering more fully from the disease.

New Tiny Battlefields

It is hoped that the fight against polio is entering its endgame. However, what might prevent this happening and where could new polio battlegrounds emerge?

A New Strain

The polio virus can mutate and if this happens, the current vaccine may not be effective. Scientists have already identified three different strains but should a fourth one develop, it could be a new battlefield. The Enterovirus 71 causes similar symptoms to polio and, like polio, it has no known cure. From the late 1990s, there have been outbreaks of the virus in the Asia-Pacific region. The virus can affect the hands, feet, and mouth and, in extreme cases, it can also impair brain activity.

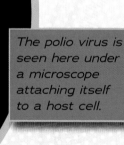

The polio virus is seen here under a microscope attaching itself to a host cell.

AFFORDABLE VACCINES

WHO is in the process of setting up factories to produce the polio vaccine in developing countries so that they are more in control of vaccinating their citizens in a sustainable and affordable way. For the world to remain polio free, immunization has to continue and be part of every country's health-care program.

A FIGHTING CHANCE

There is a real chance to make medical history and for polio to become the second disease to be eradicated worldwide. For this to happen, politicians need to work closely with doctors and scientists and assist them in their work. If one person remains infected, then all people remain vulnerable.

"Nearly eradicated is not good enough . . . When we have the vaccines and tools to save children's lives, it is not good enough to wait. Because while we wait, children are dying. As long as one child remains at risk, all children remain at risk, and that isn't a risk we can take . . . few ideas are more powerful than the eradication of human disease—what is missing is the political will to see it through. Let us eradicate polio once and for all."

David Cameron,
prime minister of the United Kingdom

43

CAN WE WIN THE WAR?

For the first time in human history, a polio-free future seems to be within reach. Political will, medical expertise, and education have eradicated the devastating virus in all but a few places in the world.

WORKING TOGETHER

In 1988, Albert Sabin developed an oral polio vaccine, which is still in use today. This vaccine has reduced polio worldwide by 99 percent. If polio is eradicated, it will be one of the greatest global medical triumphs of all time. It will be proof that science, technology, politics, and people can work together for the betterment of human life.

A global eradication of polio will transform the lives of children worldwide.

LATEST NEWS

India is just months away from being declared polio-free by WHO. This is extraordinary in a country with a population of more than 1 billion people. Nigeria, Pakistan, and Afghanistan remain polio endemic, with their neighboring countries on alert for outbreaks. With conflict areas adding to the polio case count, it is now a critical time to ensure that mass immunization takes place in the remaining polio strongholds before the virus spreads farther still.

"My ambition was to bring to bear on medicine a chemical approach. I did that by chemical manipulation of viruses and chemical ways of thinking in biomedical research."

Jonas Salk

FIGHT TO THE DEATH

The human body has strong defenses and can protect itself against many infections. However, it cannot defend itself on its own from the deadly polio virus. Humans do not have natural immunity to the virus, so they must use the medical weapons at their disposal if they are to have a chance of fighting the disease. The world stands on the brink of victory. The war against the polio virus is slowly being won, but the outcome of the final battle is yet to be decided.

With continued effort, images of polio victims such as this one will slowly become a feature of the past.

GLOSSARY

BACTERIA microscopic, single-celled lifeforms

CENTRAL NERVOUS SYSTEM the cells and spinal cord nerves that control body functions

CONTAGIOUS easily passed from one person to another through direct contact

ENDEMIC regularly found among people in a particular area

EPIDEMIC a fast-spreading disease

ERADICATE to destroy or completely get rid of something

IMMOBILIZED prevented from moving

IMMUNE SYSTEM the body's way of recognizing and fighting cells, objects, and organisms that are not part of itself

IMMUNIZED made resistant to disease, usually by vaccination

INFRASTRUCTURE a system of organization for public services such as transportation or health care

INOCULATE to protect someone from disease by giving them a weakened form of it in order for the body to create immunity to the disease

MENINGITIS a serious, sometimes fatal disease caused by a virus or bacterial infection in the brain and spinal cord membrane

MOTOR NEURON a cell that carries messages from the brain or spinal cord to the muscles

MUTATES changes or evolves

NEURAL PATHWAYS the ways neurons link to muscle function

PARALYSIS temporary or permanent loss of movement due to nerve or muscle damage

RECEPTORS nerve endings

SPINAL TAP inserting a needle into the spinal cord to get a sample of fluid for analysis

VACCINE a low dose of a disease given to a person to allow the immune system to produce antibodies against the disease

VIROLOGIST a scientist who studies viruses

For More Information

Books

Krohn, Katherine. *Jonas Salk and the Polio Vaccine* (Inventions and Discovery). Mankato, MN: Capstone Press, 2007.

Lew, Kristi. *How Scientists Research Cells* (Cells: The Building Blocks of Life). New York, NY: Chelsea House Publishing, 2011.

Orr, Tamara. B. *Polio* (Epidemics and Society). New York, NY: Rosen Central, 2010.

Websites

Read some personal stories of children with polio at:
www.poliochildren.org

Check out UNICEF's website to find out more about polio and what the UN is doing to fight the disease at:
www.unicef.org/immunization/polio

Find out what is happening near you or what you can do to help eradicate polio at:
www.polioeradication.org

Look at WHO's list of 10 facts on polio eradication at:
www.who.int/features/factfiles/polio

INDEX